Sounds All Around Us

How Do We Hear?

Charlotte Guillain

Heinemann
LIBRARY

www.heinemannlibrary.co.uk
Visit our website to find out more information about Heinemann Library books.

To order:

☎ Phone +44 (0) 1865 888066
🖨 Fax +44 (0) 1865 314091
💻 Visit www.heinemannlibrary.co.uk

Heinemann is an imprint of Capstone Global Library Limited, a company incorporated in England and Wales having its registered office at 7 Pilgrim Street, London, EC4V 6LB – Registered company number: 6695582

"Heinemann" is a registered trademark of Pearson Education Limited, under licence to Capstone Global Library Limited

Edited by Charlotte Guillain, Rebecca Rissman, and Catherine Veitch
Designed by Joanna Hinton-Malivoire
Original illustrations © Capstone Global Library Ltd
Illustrations: Tony Wilson (p. 12–16)
Picture research by Tracy Cummins and Tracey Engel
Originated by Heinemann Library
Printed by South China Printing Company Limited

ISBN 978 0 431 19337 3 (hardback)
13 12 11 10 09
10 9 8 7 6 5 4 3 2 1

British Library Cataloguing in Publication Data
Guillain, Charlotte
How do we hear? - (Sounds all around us)
612.8'5
A full catalogue record for this book is available from the British Library.

Acknowledgements
The author and publishers are grateful to the following for permission to reproduce copyright material: Alamy pp. **4 top left** (©UpperCut Images), 6 (©Hemis), 10 (©Patrick Steel), 11 (©Mihaela Ninic), 17 (©WoodyStock), 19 (©Human Nature), 21 (©AfriPics.com), **23b** (©Human Nature); Getty Images pp. 18 (©Photographer's Choice/Adrian Pope), 20 (©Visuals Unlimited/Reinhard Dirscherl); iStockPhoto pp **4 bottom right** (©Peeter Viisimaa), **4 top right** (©Frank Leung), 7 (©Ahmad Faizal Yahya), 8 (©ManoAfrica), **23c** (©Frank Leung), **23d** (©Ahmad Faizal Yahya); Photolibrary pp. 5 (©Stockbyte), 9 (©PureStock); Shutterstock p. **4 bottom left** (©devi).

Cover photograph of a boy whispering into a girl's ear reproduced with permission of Getty Images (©Steve Satushek). Back cover photograph of a desert lynx (caracal) reproduced with permission of Photo Library (©Pure Stock).

The publishers would like to thank Nancy Harris and Adriana Scalise for their assistance in the preparation of this book.

Every effort has been made to contact copyright holders of any material reproduced in this book. Any omissions will be rectified in subsequent printings if notice is given to the publisher.

Contents

Sounds

There are many different sounds.

We hear different sounds around us every day.

What are sounds?

Sounds make the air shake,
or vibrate.

sound wave

When the air vibrates it is called a sound wave.

Ears

sound wave

Sound waves travel through the air.

Animals need ears to hear
sound waves.

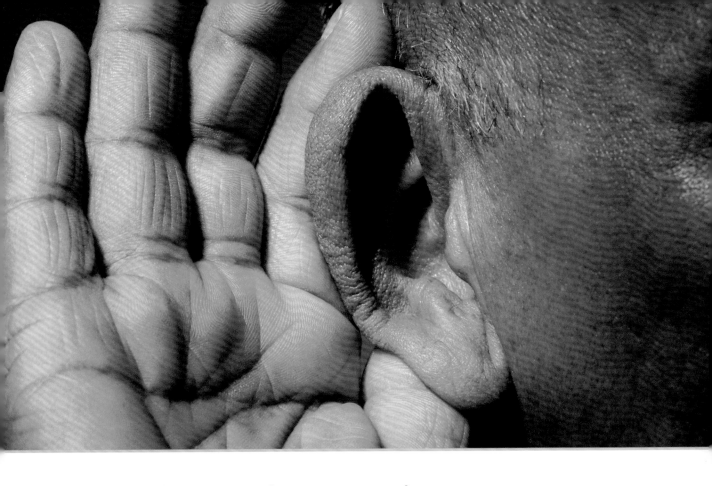

People need ears to hear
sound waves.

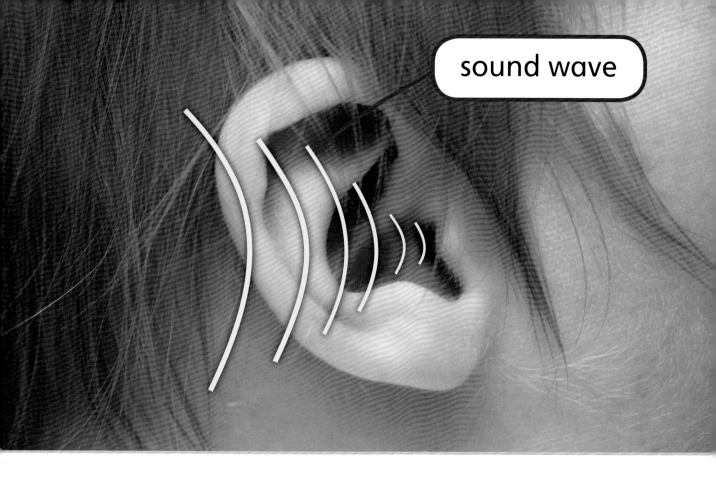

sound wave

People need ears to catch
sound waves.

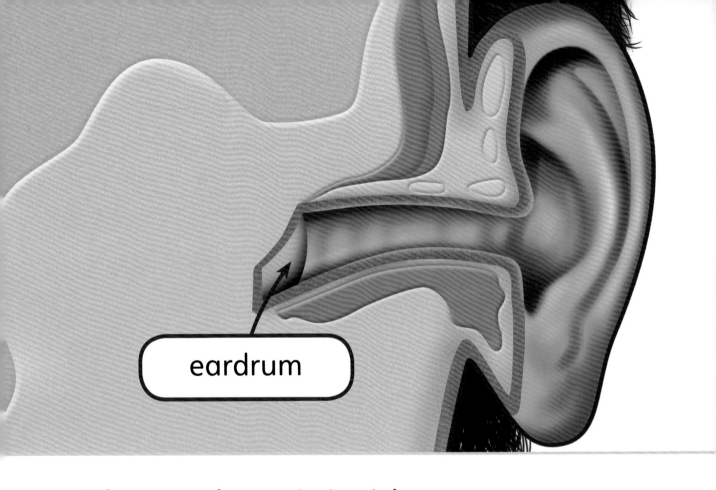

eardrum

The eardrum is inside our ear.

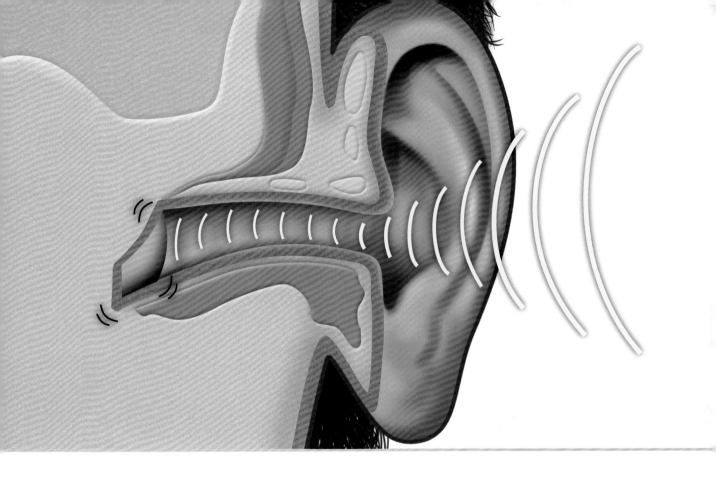

Sound waves make the
eardrum vibrate.

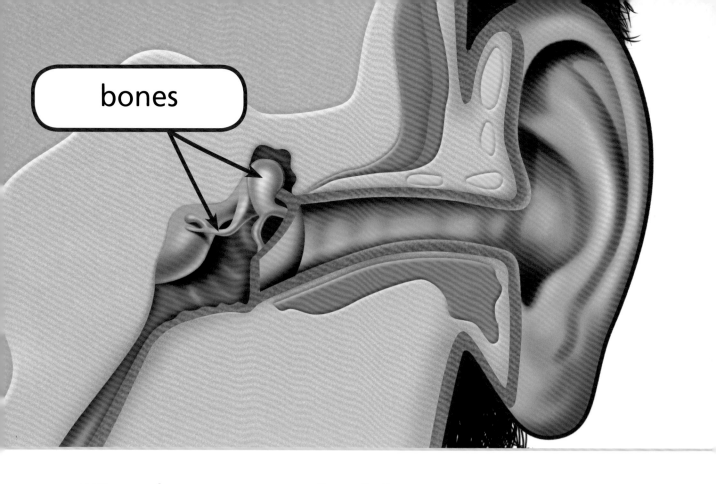

bones

Tiny bones are inside our ear.

Picture glossary

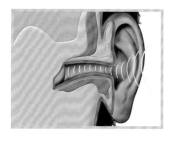

eardrum part inside your ear that shakes when sound hits it

sense something that helps you smell, see, touch, taste, and hear things around you

sound wave when the air shakes very quickly

vibrate shake very quickly

Index

Note to parents and teachers
Before reading
Tell the children that every day we make and hear sounds all around us. Explain that sounds make the air vibrate and that when the air vibrates, it makes sound waves. Tell the children that our ears catch the sound waves and that is how we hear sounds.

After reading
• Make a chart with the children about the sounds they hear everyday.
• Create a basic diagram of the ear for each child. Work as a class to label the different parts of the ear.
• Discover how people use their senses by reading My Five Senses by Aliki.